RAIN IN PLURAL

.

PRINCETON SERIES OF CONTEMPORARY POETS

Susan Stewart, series editor

For other titles in the Princeton Series of Contemporary Poets see page 109

RAIN IN PLURAL

Poems

Fiona Sze-Lorrain

PRINCETON UNIVERSITY PRESS
Princeton & Oxford

Requests for permission to reproduce material from this work
  should be sent to permissions@press.princeton.edu

Published by Princeton University Press
41 William Street, Princeton, New Jersey 08540
6 Oxford Street, Woodstock, Oxfordshire OX20 1TR

press.princeton.edu

Library of Congress Cataloging-in-Publication Data
Name: Sze-Lorrain, Fiona, author.
Title: Rain in plural : poems / Fiona Sze-Lorrain.
Description: Princeton : Princeton University Press, [2020] | Series: Princeton series of
  contemporary poets | Includes bibliographical references.
Identifiers: LCCN 2020002304 (print) | LCCN 2020002305 (ebook) | ISBN 9780691203584
  (hardback : acid-free paper) | ISBN 9780691203560 (paperback) | ISBN 9780691203577
  (ebook)
Classification: LCC PS3619.Z44 R35 2020 (print) | LCC PS3619.Z44 (ebook) DDC
  811/.6–dc23
LC record available at https://lccn.loc.gov/2020002304
LC ebook record available at https://lccn.loc.gov/2020002305

British Library Cataloging-in-Publication Data is available

Editorial: Anne Savarese and Jenny Tan
Production Editorial: Ellen Foos
Text Design: Pamela Schnitter
Cover Design: Pamela Schnitter
Production: Erin Suydam
Publicity: Jodi Price and Katie Lewis
Copyeditor: Jodi Beder

Grateful acknowledgment is made for permission to reprint excerpts from the following previously
  published material:

Reprinted by permission of Kodansha USA, Inc. Excerpted from *Basho: The Complete Haiku*,
  by Jane Reichhold. Copyright © 2008, 2013 by Jane Reichhold.

"Rain" by Gu Cheng, from *Sea of Dreams: The Selected Writings of Gu Cheng*, copyright © 1980
  by Gu Cheng, translation copyright © 2005 by Joseph R. Allen. Reprinted by permission of
  New Directions Publishing Corp.

Inscription on Plato's door, probably at the Academy at Athens, from the *Oxford Treasury of Sayings
  and Quotations*, edited by Susan Ratcliffe. Copyright © 2011 by Oxford University Press.
  Reproduced with permission of Oxford Publishing Limited through PLSclear.

"Discovered," in *We Women*, by Edith Södergran, translated by Samuel Charters. Copyright © 2015
  by Samuel Charters. Reprinted by permission of Tavern Books.

"Desolation Row" written by Bob Dylan. Copyright © 1965 by Warner Bros. Inc.; renewed 1993
  by Special Rider Music.

Cover art: Howard Hodgkin, *Déjà vu, Déjà Blue*, 2004, oil on wood © The Estate of Howard
  Hodgkin. Courtesy of Gagosian.

This book has been composed in Adobe Garamond Pro and Scala Sans

Printed on acid-free paper. ∞

Printed in the United States of America

10 9 8 7 6 5 4 3 2 1

CONTENTS

in summer rain
the leg of the crane
becomes shorter

BASHŌ

Raising our colorful placards toward the sky
we protest against this sort of sorrow

GU CHENG

I

CLOSER TO CLOUDS

MORE VULNERABLE THAN OTHERS

So what if I break

I will continue to eat mud

unwind underground

        mask banned signs

chew holes in every tall grapevine

      breed my roots after a nap

spread fronds as free

        clothes free money

lay branches bare for the moon and its jaws

      while each flower falls

to its own bad dream

WALKING OUT ON THE LYRIC

When men take from me all the heat and light, I content myself
      with echoes, sounds, and radio waves in every room up for sale inside

this body. What's gone stretches each wall so terribly that when
      I cough, mud bricks give up their secrets and poor decisions. One

of the corners keeps the song alive, another too wet for dust
      or sprigs to rot gently. I manage. Each furniture piece makes its

long speech to accept my dual friendship: one from France,
      the other to inherit an armoire. To obey an inner despot, I check

the doors, sweep the balcony, and reframe each picture with clouds
      or perfect fruits as focus. For inspiration, I look out the windows.

I am inside each window, the window moves in me. Anything you see
      from the outside—the garden, the hare, disposable bin, and wayfaring

tree—teaches you to live with used spaces. Touch pain by its rim:
      under your bed, in the cellar. I am still here because of my dilemma.

In this scenario, a glass of water and a pill are two separate issues.
      Look at you. The solitude. Even the cactus is softening each kill.

MACABRE DANCE

On a night like this, I hear the spirit
in simple three-four beat. Even if my heart
gets tired believing. Almost naked,
standing in a barn. Now I understand
before and after giving. *Da capo,*
if the voice survives. Anxiety
and my navel trying to open
like a foolish eye. Sight and touch,
two battles to fight. I watch
the blur of a gray horizon shift
before dividing into two feral
zones. Coil a sash around
my groin to heal the snake in me,
slow passing of joy, in the midst
of ripeness. Of lust. Of reason.
Of penitence. Nipples large
and eager to please. With remorse
and quick glory. Moonlight loses
its greasy flex. The air smells young
but unsafe. I think of a one-legged
poet who brews glutinous rice wine
and writes about black goats
giving birth in the mountain heat.
Well-behaved in a fauve landscape—
among poppies and nomads who feed
them shamefully. Goats do not prepare
for rain or transition. They stand near
the graves because of their safeguard.

Waves toss in their eyes before sleep
or exercise. Helpless in a world where
the spirit moves the real. Where rain
tastes like a drug and is seen air by air.

THE PROBLEM WITH MUSIC

I broke my guzheng, string by string.
Yells
in astral mode, down
a spongy hill
or God knows what splendid,
historic cliff.
Snow did not come to mind
when my feet
expected it. Suddenly
clean, the idea
of acting
versus its ideology.
I watched the aria with a deep
breath, from
a source of torture.
I did nothing.
Telling myself I must do nothing.

A MATTER OF TIME

in memoriam C.K.S. (192?–2013)

The last time I saw this body, this body
chose me. "Fiona," it called out
loud at sundown, and I remember
nothing of what I did. Sometimes I bent close
to check if it breathed.
In-between scenes a thousand
miles from this ward, crowded yet receding,
days when air was still clear—a little raw
—a village, primary colors, the kitchen

where I memorized idioms and T'ao Ch'ien
and love poems, sesame cakes, Shanghainese
dumplings to steam with napa cabbage,
a stone house gone in flames on her sixtieth
birthday. What's left behind of the field
reminds me of this body. A wounded
horse which must suffer in order to live.
Rubble fresh and set apart from the disaster.
The body is fighting with the spirit inside it.
What would the flesh say? Nothing,

it says. It says nothing. Now I touch its skin,
the cream of being alive, in decorum, after
three lives four countries in nine decades.
The past and the present against what
comes next. Four daughters to consult
the book and a son abroad. Sweetly
or briefly, the impressive cruelty. If soul

can't talk to body, each organ to vie
for prayer before victory, is there,

is there—I can't invent this lack
of a last word. Help me with the title,
not in words or grief or all of it opening
to seek relief. "Never stay politically
naive," the voice returns
to colonize my fury. In the end
the beginning unnecessary, to avoid
anguish. Grandmother.
Two women.
Facing exhaustion without permission to leave.

TASTE THE SUN,

said my grandmother.

Each warm bun with a silver star inside.
Clouds descended to feed the fable.

I wanted to keep it on my tongue.
The star, not the sun.

A chimeric flavor. *Of course,*

she added, *if you close your eyes*
and lick the circle back and front.

[Threads of stellar wind—conjunctive—

two matching spheres—in disbelief—one

more bite—I relish—source data—a mystic

screen—her journal—loud—within]

WHAT I SAW WHEN I LOOKED OUT THE WINDOW OF A CLAIRVOYANT HOUSE

Back in a place that had lost its relic,
I asked a monk to reclock the emptiness. He showed me how
                                to leave each window outside.
I told him I saw three spirits at predawn.
Maimed by their own hands, like
in a Neolithic culture.

Something the monk said about the mangrove ferns
and the gouache print of a hill
made me recall
a lost world from Kuching.

The house and its will,
soon to converse like neighbors.

I didn't take its trust for granted.

Instead of cleaning up, I worked around its scent.

Instead of waiting for my husband to clean it up, I burned sweetgrass

after an elliptical prayer—noun A, noun B,
                                and a passive-active verb—
in a secular vault where I thought the three spirits
would eat my dinner cold,
recycle their fear,
and make peace as mortals.

Instead of a fawn and grazing horse, I saw the mother deer
licking sugar from a sack.

Instead of a stranger, I heard a bicycle.

Instead of letters, I dropped October:
night one/day two, a visible deadweight.

A fight in Montana ended a weak pact. Freed me of this
flood and basement—
                    it wasn't a grotto or some dry creekbed,
but a well into which a virgin concubine
threw herself to save her story,
and haunt and grieve our hellish footsteps.

ARIOSO

Fingers are thinking like the Peranakan queen
    who takes a morning stroll with shoulder-high creepers.

TO THE TUNE OF ONE VALLEY

Here comes a white note a blind
poet can trust.   A legend

      without limbs, but pleased
      to give its heart—

I arrive earlier
than ash and songbirds,

breakfast settled with legs   in full-lotus:

planning to witness its exit and clouding,
      to prolong the crawl

between one surprise
and the next flashlight. Immanence
        and transcendence: the liturgy
is stretched by a vixen.   Sunset watcher, all mountains

are ways of rain. Even
      in nonviolence, it is wise to break

through the whole picture. Distance nailed,
I recall your sonnet—

   bell, pebble, a bouquet
   on our roof
   to unfurl few regrets,

part of mystery, O half   this journey,

untamed by what we see, or where
questions have lived.

AFTER BEING LOVED

"Someone ought to come
more often than usual," says the concierge
who worships Monica Vitti
and leaves the mail on my doormat before
I answer her. If not for the door, light
would be sentenced to life without parole.
Judged and demented down each passage.
I am pulling through a hard
November, not breathing enough
to sleep or work on kindness. From this balcony
the piazza smells like a dying consort. She
thinks of lovers in dynasties
and battles, anywhere
but here until their exile is over.
A granddaughter of the Sinn Féin will visit
tomorrow: she is bringing a ladle
and sausage, and can advise me on a stanza
by Blake, *And mutual fear brings peace, / Till
the selfish loves increase: / Then Cruelty
knits a snare, / And spreads his baits with care.*
"Campaigners," she quipped
last year, "wait for the media
and jump to conclusions."
Lunch to prepare after feeling stronger.
An hour of moxibustion and Italian verbs:
essere, avere, potere, devere . . .
A chain novel from the postwar era.
Old footage, never lack of impostors.
Stillness like this to erase

better: nothing has happened, the break flawless.
Over a nightgown I put on my coat, leave the apartment
and walk without focus. Reading statues
or tourists, strangers in the middle of longing and speech.

PREFACE TO A CLOUD CHRONICLE

Copious wind: a birthright exerting its violence.
Dance with sleeve gestures, like in the Central Plain.
Tree ferns thinning in rough times.
A rabbit from the woods.
Looking for a park to die.
Two servants clear fruits from a blue altar.
A sheriff on his way to the temple.
Vile letter, right before dinner.
Kant, Donne, and Burke: in this democracy.
Then, Kazuo (first name) Dan (last name).
Osamu Dazai (pen name) for another time.
Herbal soup—not to mix with rice.
All-male kabuki for a news bulletin.
No rewrite. A Garbo to deny.
No, Garbo would deny.
Black noodles—scoop out the beef tongue.
Marriage arranged for a boat festival.
Livelier birds atop a tree due to the nerve
of one widow's flashback. Quietly, her future.
A long cane chair, to sit through a self-inflicted burn.
Low twilight.
Low expectations.
Soak my feet, finger each breath.
Watch the lake grow its spleen and stomach
and a sudden rouge in a soft lifespan.

REINCARNATED, BUT NOT FOR THE FIRST TIME

This happens when I'm ready for my own flesh.

If only the world were as spacious and precise as such a moment,

I wouldn't need outlaws and my goddamned pride,
I'd be able to fix the smooth decline.

HAS IT BEEN EIGHT MONTHS

In my head, a coffin portrait:

not the one taken in a cheesy studio, but the one my father thought it best to see her
    through bardo
even though she said she couldn't stand the experience
    of transition—each lamp

in each eye smothered in its own time, while we upped

the dose of something I couldn't spell. It has been eight

months
her portrait eats my lungs, not
    when I pant but when my taste buds rotate to mourn
and fast. It has been eight months

I know her portrait
    is contagious as hell: once I see her nose and lips, I think of nothing else

but a defaced coin, clay kettle, two scandalous lines by Pasolini.

It has been eight months I multiply anger in my hair, solar
    plexus, and house plant,

each day an orchid,
each month a depression to figure out her smile.

FAR FROM DESCRIPTION

Day after day,
this sentence grew longer. The verb ran faster

than expected. Pushy

as ever, it hurt the feelings of its own

speaker.
I was the speaker who couldn't agree with its mood—it wasn't grief,

ecstasy, or fury
I experienced when pregnant with a rebel. It

was the way a regret

lingered—stuck and turning in one corner,

as if it couldn't perish without being heard,
as if its madness drove me to silence,
as if reason
or the sound of it mattered.

SMALL STORMS

TO SUFFERING, TO LIBERATION

I address you not as twin sisters,

> but as two fruits hanging from the same branch of a tree
> planted by an agnostic farmer. He prayed for harvest in October,
> asked for a wife
> season after season, coveting the life

> of a painter who drew from scratch
> a still life of two pears in a basket—
> simple but climactic,
> they looked equal

yet dissimilar, recognized by him who planted their tree.

MIMESIS: CLOUD CHRONICLE

   after Sankai Juku

    The stage went dark.
Odes were smuggled. Twelve sheer basins gleamed
not for joy, but for each spirit to outlast
its shrine. Cloaked in white, dancers lay
            in a fetal position,
then buoyed up
their torsos and gasped. Faces blank, they gawked
at themselves. No one came, not even foreigners.
      Was this wakefulness?
      Or an illusion, a dream in a dream—in which bodies
rose, cut off from their dream truth
and mirror world?

The scene was slow, a pseudo-climax. Hijikata the founder
counted on the dead to enact the downfall
of a psychic whole. I should have said
      reenact: to objectify
the ritual and its site,
a dialogue with the earth against the carnal.
Years gone, this act stands: a dancer
stirred as if he had stomached a tomb,
      an internalized film running day and night,
an intelligence rid of argument, that
he was neither a body
nor gesture—*it* was a tree, a reason, a vertical creature
that stopped to suffer, even when moving in praise of the spirit.

11

Front-page headline: humans renew
their happiness every twelve years. Eleven the integer
observes a freedom more theological
than impartial, the promise of likeness
and a portrait of balance. Based on lottery
instead of trial and error,
my theory about joie de vivre estimates
the costs of a godsend parcel.
Come 2001, the year I fell ill. Twice hospitalized
without insurance. Got over Emma Goldman
and "The Jewish Giant." Scared of making
love, I wore a *vierge moderne*,
spied on a beggar who stole my foil
blade and selfhood. Read Nostradamus
in an unheated museum
when I should have turned in fifty words
on Montesquieu. Three nights I mouthed
felonies by Goneril, understudied
lust for a hell staged in *King Lear*.
Come September eight, nine,
ten, and twelve—
a priest lost control over a confession,
the clock maimed its hands.
Those mornings I had handled with sangfroid
via sixty-five percent high-fiber breakfasts.
Threw gloves to the cat and cooked
barley water, unsugared to curb
the malevolent soot.
Sun, did you brave the world as projected?

Lord, bring me faith that will free
me from fear of being caught in a sniper scope.
I was spared from harm by a quiz on Beckett.
Spared, I mourn the prime number without its facts learned.

A FROZEN REQUIEM

That the graveyard of a vision could be seen

before the vision stopped short at the water's edge.

FROM A WINTER THAT ISN'T A REHEARSAL BUT THE FIRST SEQUENCE OF ATONAL PITCHES

I accept the truth in newspapers
by holding the murder of my friends against my chest.

To each weather forecast I give thanks:
merci for every outdated

dusk/dawn. More terror, more pressing pollution . . .
By chance, Voltaire is dropped

from a school curriculum. Cancer
the horoscope sails on free waters. In France, theaters suffer

worse than asylums. Grueling times,
grueling politics. Tax-free plants. Agritourism. Air

and butterflies on a slimming diet. My husband
hires a lawyer for his will. *She won't*

be wealthy, the latter claims, *but she'll be safe,*
it'd be alright. Fine—doubts my soul

before a rash move. In each flower
the evil seeks exoneration, *Winter now, I'm the rare one*

who blossoms, don't you see the fight I defend? January,
I praise you for this cold garden:

wind disfigures each death the earth pockets from trees,
each bench empty for the next couple.

THE REALITY OF A NIGHTMARE

At any second the rooster could have crowed three times.
JORGE LUIS BORGES

A man with a gun moved the piano

from my hindbrain into my chest.

Inch by inch, my bed shortened its waking state. Potatoes I ate
    for supper laughed.

Faces melted
into kisses between pigs. Dressed
        in pajamas with eyes shut, they tiptoed
        in Derby shoes,
        dreaming of an abattoir now a church.

WOLINSKI 1934–2015

I praise laughter, its hairy torso and tattooed fingers.
Rated positions from the *Kama Sutra*—I could have drawn some
     in one clean stroke.
Think of my women as open umbrellas, wired to jazz with Lady Ella.
I leave a cat out of the picture.
Heroes brush their teeth and read graffiti.
                                   O writers who partied
against our prize, let me raise a glass to your first-rate Greek.

NEVER ONCE

After visiting a museum igloo with three Italian friends, one of them
                                          a world-class bridge player
After Heidegger in five hours
After a casserole of black pepper crabs, fished out of a musical aquarium
After dining with a league of prime brokers, a poet from Taiwan on her best behavior
After hanging up on silence
After an entente between your ancestors, your son
                          and daughter, your biological weapons
After deciding not to become our own parents
After our failure to stay as brothers and sisters
After Kafka, his vegetarian meals
After Moravia
      or his difficult women (who each became an artist in her
                                          own right)
After scouting for the best laksa in London
After Lithuania
After loving your neighbors, the diabolical heaven
After the first two houses and a transit between two wealth-giving planets
After a long sale
After my favorite samurai
After the matchmaker who studied owls
After a cello rhapsody, the "Dying Swan" by Plisetskaya
After an easy pregnancy, an easier insomnia
After the postwar value system
                    and a more documented abdication
After our dim sum
            at Shangri-La, even though the oolong tea was served while we quarreled
After an eviction, not a hurricane
After Pope Francis, the year twenty-thirteen

After reaching different planes of existence during an induced sleep

                                           for science and mainstream journalism

After the dismissal of a caregiver

After listening to the last stretch of Callas: her aria and its antipositivism

After a duel in Umbria, in which the maestro lost his secret

After nonthought/nonaction via a nonself/nonmoment—preferably with some emotion

After every king, his children, and their revised list

       of queens, plays, and errors

After *after, après, dopo* . . .

                       in English, the word was used before the Middle Ages, the fall

of Rome

and a wound open to interpretation—

34

SELF-RELIANCE

To rebirth a tree that weeps in my womb,
        I heal anger with flower essences: aspen, white chestnut, and mustard.

Two pencils in each pocket.

Hysteria and euphoria equal a patent storm. Euphoria and hysteria
                                                    equal a latent gene.

The negative of each sentence isn't its translation.
        1. The negative of a portrait picture revives a life in two worlds. *True or false*
        2. The negative of a memory can be exposed within hours. *True or false*
        3. The negative of any number takes into account an emotion. *True or false*

Read about Snowden. Think about his country *based on a true story.*

I exist as a color
every other year, a recipe per season.

Rain—rain—rain. Yes: no, yes.

Due to my budget, Brecht and Puccini cost less than the phone bill.

Femininity: a desire to lead.

In his obituary, Plato qualifies *green politics.*

Zero is a state of being and becoming. One takes a long time
                                                    to get used to it.

accept the strangeness evasion a magnetic oval an abrupt derailment accept the newly tested drugs reclassified data about teeth lungs fingernails the radioactive tub an inquisitor's rundown amateur astronomy commercial fishing the cultural impact of astrology Korean sushis Japanese wines accept the semantic pull of "hairdresser" "anthologize" "suitcase" "eclipse" "moral risk"

Earn your catharsis after each night shift. Foot massage. Virtual sex. This isn't the last of Communism.

Have you listened to Clapton the guitarist
         instead of Clapton the rock artist? You don't have to fantasize.
         You don't need to drink.

Reprisal. To demonize dissent. A patriot checked "Y" for all the questions.

I know the patriot but not his family. His family doesn't know where he lives.

I feel braver about infinity.

I am visible between two mothers. We are creating between liberties.

ODE TO DISAPPOINTMENT

How well you perform each post-
        failure gag, in the thick of nightmares
                or relieved heartburn, a swan song
        of always yet never, sooner than later,
the quicker the better. Trust is raped,

I weep for a new bride. Drained
        of speech, you free the last sentence.
                Gone for a weekend, you return
        with a man in two novels: a father
from some past or a husband who decides.

Vague as usual, in terms of conclusion.
        To claim a sorry, deliver your proof
                of absolution. Mailed overnight,
        sealed by nonspecific tears. I'm afraid
of your Aristotelian violence: is life

but a dream or sensory wisdom; are
        we a unity of time, place, and action?
                Be my muse. Be my flame and tranquilizer—
        don't go yet. Don't despair. I won't
steal your breath and your shine.

TO CRITICS

who dig up a word or clause from its grave,
expose its antipodal
limbs, pick at the bones (their chemical
            truths): don't
you fiddle with my heroine who looks
            to the dawn as "awakening" (on her train to seventh heaven
before a natural catastrophe).
I take you seriously.
                My clichés: men (or women essayists)
who smoke Davidoff and travel
to Venice—to visit Brodsky's tomb or make peace with a foul
part of themselves,
peering through a window from the Bridge of Sighs.
Adjectives that manhandle a range
of emotions, fit to be converted to even digits.
I've folded into two, four, eight, twelve . . .

a list of your woes,
cast each lot into a sea of credo
and conscience. I believe in exclamation marks: they
wink at an upheaval.
            Jealous of French words, do you trust
them with a mission? I spend
hours weighing their goodwill
in a café run by feminists in East London.
Je est un autre, how—the music
leaves it out in cut time. Nostalgia
for the sublime is reformed
by a quill. (I bought it
            from a Milanese hooker.) Speaking of Milan,

none of my fados about her glamour
makes the most of *The Last Supper*.
This litany is ashamed of derision; forgive me

before I worsen. Look not for an aperture,
but a hole where mice revolt
                when the cat appears.
My house has a rug in every room.
Doors think harder when you knock.
A home away from the desert, the kite. (I couldn't begin
with a less obvious idiom.)
            O summer, thine affective fallacy—
what should flowers do in spite of what they are onscreen.
            Soul capitalized, I confirm.
Can't we gender countries
or fountains, but leave dependent territories,
reefs, oxbow lakes androgynous?
I save commas like saving up pennies.
(Christa) Wolf, not (Virginia) Woolf.
Here comes an email. Let's not
fight over a possessive for love. Best,

LOOSE CLOUD CHRONICLES

I   Far from Manhattan

December 1998

Because they have never met in real life, he tries to detect
her psyche, studying her
handwriting from the envelope—
poems he sent her return
with ticks and notes scrawled
across verses, in a pen pressure soft
enough to break silence. Most letters contain
a forward slant, which he mistakes as a mood
swing in winter. Spacing between words isn't
too modest, but assures one of a fair
distance. Tied in gentle knots
with winding downstrokes, her cursive f
nourishes his fantasy: the solitude
that fuels her fiction whispers for a man,
a happier life without a garden.

Over time her j misses its dot.
Ceilings that sag inside her apartment?
Three months after, her I
stands more erect, confrontational, yet its darkened
ink bares a hooded mind, the map
of a labyrinth its grasp
of an ocean. He wishes he could toss
into its waves fossils, rain,
then lanes, sunsets, taverns, sandwiches,
illegible bills. The fear of drowning is a continent
from here. Nothing hinders a sequel

where it must function. He picks up a crayon,
finds a tea stain smeared on his work,
and scribbles on it, *Chère Marguerite I know it hurts*—
no indent or comma, only an imagined
air to listen, a phrase that comforts with a free
hand at the end, pursed lips hum the "Emperor"
concerto, reaching a high D and an erotic trill,
before he signs off in the skeleton of a treble clef.

    for and after Natasha Sajé

II   Via Manzoni, Milano

September 2010

Without reason, the street chopped
                    off its own arms—we lost
and found one another, looking
      for its fingers. In a bright piazza, he stopped
for music, the absolute
      silence mimed in a pianist's gestures.
      No one but us knew
he had shadowed

      into a gray region, another aspect
of breath,
weight, and grace. Like a chandelier he swayed, this
      way and that. So tastefully that
he went unnoticed, at the center
of a hub
ready to travel—false emergencies, the worst

      traffic, love lyrics that rhymed
(and unrhymed), a palazzo
(more palazzi), an oxygen bar, overcooked
      zuppa with a midwife for dinner . . . My brother

began his optimism
from a shuttered villa, a seedy
        parlor with baby charioteers, bourgeois mothers,

and the nouveau riche from different *città*. They applauded
        each contender, even when a piece
ran amok. Philippe asked how a rondo must end.
I don't know.
Perhaps without an end.
        Il mio maestro del sogno—
he who sought partitas, yoga, and Da Vinci,
        told us *The moon suffered a breakdown,*
and still waltzed.

III   After Thirty Years, a Fortune Teller

        May 2013

Dodging a judgment or an opinion, she stared
                        at a tree (Yes, you're the tree)
        or another man *(Are you still he?)*
on Boulevard Routine,
                on his way to a factory.

Most afternoons, she seemed less violent.
I filled up her refrigerator
        with lemons and eggs, left the gingerbread "Voronezh" in a basket.

From her balcony, she protested
the daily life—
                a dog's shadow under the red flag,
                        a stoic setting sun
and its sanctioned clouds.

Hopeful, but is that good enough?

Silence no longer an invisible gift,
        spared by a speechless clock in the toilet.

Listen to what Ludmila B. failed to break. Listen to how she said her grace
and tried to sleep.

STRAND

Three nights before his death, I described the sweetness
        of his tortilla de patatas to a stranger
who became my neighbor, a singer whose ears looked pointed but not elvish
enough to trigger a blank verse, and that was three nights

before his death when I hit it off with her, after salting potatoes
and half a dozen eggs
to cook a tortilla in the shape of Manhattan, a meal that Kafka
        his favorite atheist
would have pictured as healthy but way too pleasant.

DUENDE

They say the last to sleep will relive
each feast: the glee of white
dwarfs, a labor that runs deep. I have always thought this
      is how stars arrive,

one brighter than others,
its solitude
kicking, not to make a fuss, but to hold and slow the trance.

III

NINE SOLITUDES

Hills fidget when clouds are painted to make them scream. For a betrayal nothing stays literal. The core of each lie grows against its skin in a color so grainy and chaste that it lures you to touch it, dress by dress. I listen to the dial tones when I phone my enemies. Viscous at some point, then predatory. There is always time to discern their tension. Why they speak of their childhood is beyond my grip. Know how it feels to be judged and made useless: your name is a tree felled by a half-ton shear, each howl jinxed by the onlookers' laughter. I have worked with two kinds of wind hunters: honest and sneaky. Neither asked to stay as friends after the harvest.

When notes ran without passion or insight, the music tied my limbic lobe to its wings. I memorized the chords because I believed in them—a sequence of internalized rivers and forests, two pages of reticence and their symptoms. Liszt borrowed each death from Lamartine, so we must attend to both potentials. Even the bells muted for their beauty. Grief maneuvered, a critic observed, to temper each wraith and its otherworldliness. I couldn't disagree after the concert. Walking down the aisle backstage felt the worst. Cruelty struck after the applause. I looked into the longest mirror I could find. It was time I saw, and the relief of mine. A wedding took place in my fingers when I was onstage. The man I wed wanted me clean.

At the memorial of a former tribal chief, we were told to meditate on the hours of fear, followed by nine prayers for a slain eagle. A syntactic silence grew its white iron lungs and made sure we breathed with them without their tumor. I thought of the parable of the ten lepers. I must have been brainwashed when I needed compassion. Time and the body, a diurnal tyranny. Its futility, fought by a rare few such as the chief here. Friends from his hometown behaved brutally. His family hailed his artistic trivia. *The life of almost any man possessing great gifts,* wrote Dickens, *would be a sad book to himself.* Let me add, *And his children.*

Had I taken his call at midnight, I might have caught a glimpse of what he went through, the curve of a tunnel before one reached for the brakes. Guilt, for lack of a fast acquittal. Shame, a bed on fire in my gut. He forgave me long before I dreamed of him. Last April, he cooked a meal without butter while I took pictures of his library. *Set aside time every night for your dead friend,* a therapist advised, *look at his portrait and light a candle.* She mentioned Taiji and Jewish hymns. Twice a month I gave her harp lessons. At a flea market, I bought a carpet with what I earned. Yes, I struggled to get the job done. To help a therapist with her ruminations. Had she realized too that my friend's portrait glared tall under the lamp on my bedstand. Or that I couldn't finish *The Death of Virgil.*

Let no one enter who does not know geometry.
INSCRIPTION ON PLATO'S DOOR, PROBABLY
AT THE ACADEMY AT ATHENS

When you reach the Academy of Ruins, take stock of the endings of those lives
    you left behind—
among other things, the letters you prepared,
stamped and addressed—

before passing through the moon-bone gate, shirt unbuttoned, breathing
   like a candle
on the wrong river.

This winter, I studied the sun and its flashy emblems of benevolence. It was difficult to get rid of the moon—it kept its balance between my eyes and fell ill in roundness before the solstice. Was that the cyclic existence of an intermediate body or reserve? Two physicians from Lamia wrote about this suffering. One defined it as an objective revenge. Of our cosmos upon an effable physique. At noon I gave the sun my bones to lick, glad to feel mortal before salting the bean curds. I laid hands on ways to sway heat from doctoring my five senses. How different a fire was from warmth or excitement. Star, offer me no advice or folklore. Show me why in French we call these mushrooms *trumpets of the dead.*

After a visit to Hampstead, I drafted a letter to Anna and Sigmund Freud. Handwritten in green, on scraps of rice paper. As I penned my thoughts, the radio cackled, *Bonjour Fiona, think well of your heart.* But I fell asleep after the third sentence—where did magic fade, how could a hat appear? Nothing readied me for the death of selfdom, not even drugs or the almighty Nietzsche. I was exhausted by my perfectionism. This British accent got me nowhere in Kansas. *Look at your ego. Don't pretend it isn't there.* Minus the entrance of Marquis de Sade who giggled and stumbled with a chunk of fatty meat tucked under his arm, my dream involved Sappho's hair, robe, and fear. In Gothic colors. Astronomical dead air in both ears, I wept like a schoolgirl while my belly swelled until it glowed and burned for hours.

Out in the fields, a myth grew past its radius.

I looked out from the porch and saw the child again.

Taller than reeds that had held off a storm, he ran toward the distant woods with a toy balloon. Birds, like bullets immortalized in the air. *Did you listen to the myth?* I shouted out to him when he set his balloon loose. An orange dot, wolfed in no time by the swarm of bullets.

He ran faster and faster, refusing to turn around and look at me. Voices from behind took to the road. The myth hovered. It began to claim the field and its river.

From afar, I watched the child reach the woods. He became a dot that moved when I stood still. I shouldn't have asked about the myth. I shouldn't have asked anything.

My hand isn't at home in yours.
Your hand is desire—
my hand is longing.
EDITH SÖDERGRAN

After a year of clairvoyance, the river has found its key and pebble and more than two curves to bait a drifter. In its flow the cold augury, my hands feel an unholy tickle: would a forbidden love be exposed again, in a hamlet where widows listen to sons with few hopes up? The river never weeps in broad daylight. Everything glistens—

to polish the hush—apart from the sky and a straight flight of swallows, overseeing the woodlands and our petty lives. By virtue of this timeworn river, pilgrims flock here to take chances on their souls. Nature reigns, so does the divine will. But the future, O tell me why, feels stolen, gorgeously impervious.

IV

DJANGO FONTINA

P

Swaggering to the bridge—I forget
which river—against a crowd in search

of offbeat charms
in this old-world quartier, *I am here,* you whisper, *I am not matter,*
        just this touch, your summer dress, an impulse to run,
                        a way to say five when you mean fifty,
        a stranger who shows you how to sin with two hands free.

[Lights change. The street noise stops.]

VOICE-OVER
Each sentence is worth a turn
after the bridge. Take your time, the blind poet says.

ESTAMPES

I   **Setting the Mood**

In the photograph, a dirt road

leads to a hero's grave.

In reality—
a Mongolian spring—
by the mound I saw two, three sheep
                [they moved or ate idly]
and a pond darkening in a milder sheen.

Silence freed magnetic echoes.
Lateral.
Polyphonic.
From each vertebra, disc by disc.
Heart throbbing like a cooked
jar of azaleas,
          each step I took, my embarrassment as intruder.

But ancient oaks: trembling west
and straight, no

arms to hold the wind, its face-voice-body and aura between flighty weeds.

II Puji Temple

Beitou, Taipei

That we did our best, despite the downpour, to enter
        bliss and Shingon
Buddhism—the abbot sat
on a famous chair, eyeing our wounds
with purgatorial calm,
        noninterference and his lunch fixed—

while I kowtowed to give up lust and a truck
that couldn't brake in every dream
since autumn: *full of infants and the dregs
of conscience,* I told him, expecting

a moral in return. Yet he uttered an unofficial
verse from a sutra that French intellectuals
        practice for good cheer,
praying for my health and the truck to stop
without *infants as puppets in spooky attire.*

III Matsuri

Unswept, unhealed: a Zen refuge,

so much in a need to turn
        inward and breed.

Wild lilies repent despite their explosion.

On a lotus leaf, incense ash.
Upstream a fishing line from a happy outing.

Come to the pond, frogs
        each a water priest waiting for magic.

Soon a boat
to pear trees and bamboo, carried by the wind

and bird calls, *Be well, be well*—

Everywhere a haiku you know of Buson: one
stem of holly,
smelling of the moon.

Lover and friend,

be tender.

Offer someone sanctuary under the first tree.

IV   0

after Alexey Titarenko

White by accident, white before splendor, not one
image resurrects the father-
sun, one that stays afloat, metaphysical,

denying its tyranny in my line. To spy and counterspy
on Dostoyevsky, pictorialism and the snow
that confesses. In Saint Petersburg, mothers look

away from one another's eyes, not of sorrow,
but to preserve their love.
Love that I thought we could save from the blizzard.

V   Sumatra

For years I returned to the same window
in a house facing the sea

I knew since my first flood.
Like when our pony died [a guest was riding it];
or between my wedding and a heart
surgery [both were scheduled
                            to put the past behind].

I made a bowl of sakéd ginger,
looked for a sail
in and out of its horizon, and prayed
without *Amen.*

Zero mind pollution, I sang faster.
Sometimes a feather.
A thank-you cloud.
Wind bells cautioned me about a scientific
freedom, the scoop of a sea
with past four billion years of sexuality.

Again the window with a sinful perspective.

Under the glare of a still-moving
sun, I saw stars in the sea which were not
but that glowed.
Took my time with yo-yo thoughts—
anything past libido could drift for hours,
like a real sampan
stoned in morning smog.

I ate steamed flowers and dried goji berries,
copied recipes,
circled ingredients oft-referenced.
I read *Mansfield Park.*
I reread *One Man's Bible.*
Followed by a more painless John Le Carré.
Listened to "Speak Low" instead of Gershwin.

Light poems occurred, almost
                    always before sleep.
One entitled "Thinking of Marlene,
Looking for Dietrich."
Another, "How to Recycle Short-Term Memory."

More doodles, more vintage films.
Then the famous dream.
Crooks in a gluten-free village.
Two lucid ringtones.
A green brunch alone.

Cooking is a routine joy, I wrote
in the margin, the sanctuary.
Therapy began with the window
                    [and the sea].
Of all endings, this was my favorite.
I counted my recipes, or all
                    that were left:
four hundred and two,
illustrated with colors strong enough to swim.

SEA BALLADS

I   Cyclical

When the moon is high, the sea lies ahead
                                        of its defectors.
On strike for power,

it has unearthed anarchy. Steadying itself

against grandeur and dissent. Each instant,
                        a revolution it doesn't want to miscarry.

                        Tides become round the way my womb fills itself
then empties out,

so much or little,

        according to laws of this generic ritual. This is why

the Muse

says the sea is a woman.
It can't control the moon, the clock of its humor. It must continue—
                        from a prehistoric

here—wearied not by time but the skeins
        of a tide,
                        silencing voices in twenty-eight

days, a rush of blood, a waste

of prayers. Begging for comfort when rebirth is over.

II   Making Waves Straight

Because we believe in sea cure, we allow sand to take
its grip on us—awkward glee from toes to tears all
day long. We enter each other from the inside
of this world, opal light, lighter and august.

Mystified hands from a higher order,
between our torsos wind creates a square
hideout, keeps it clean at the speed of earth-
shine. Don't mistake this for paradise. I think

of the brevity of greed and guilt and the worst kind
of redemption. Twenty bracelets, fourteen odes,
a dozen perfumes. None of us asks the jagged
clouds if an ocean outlives its abstraction.

We breathe this language from finish
to start. Live the strangeness of a painless
center, deep yet random, the moon skipping dinner,
corals limbic, jigging with colors from the west and the east.

III   Face to Face

sea; your
face
from two angles, a higher power

tier by tier, anticlockwise

beds of dust
arrows stained with corrosion
settling on a plane, transparent and won't sink

before memory, you were a silent film
a doctrine
a monsoon disowning its pact

with old centuries
crest after crest, your Dionysian acts:

tanned goddesses who crawl through infant legs

or Satan
thieves on center stage

and a famished chimpanzee brushing its teeth

IV Black Hour

The sea is exactly what it was when mountain, forest, swamp were
imperturbable enemies, and the sight of it restores the ancient fear.
EDWARD THOMAS

Where is the mirror that shines in broken light? In our earth's offering,
this sea begins from another sea. If it parts, it does not expect to fight.
It feels triangular when we settle down at night. I keep it in a box, safe
near my pillow. So that waves can string out my thoughts tide after
tide. Poets saw dragons and beasts where a wreckage should have been.
I caught lions, dark green and white. The sea, its glands, each an
authentic presage. Their breath, my haven—a disfigured kingdom.
Throne by throne, it fell prey to one-armed knights. What do you
think will happen. Soon, or soon. The exile must return.

V   Late Shower

Pared down to mist and a snare of light, the boat in your whisper lures
a plainsong out of us. Blues of a third language seeking new stories.
Lips against lips, we feel the roof and a birth so immediate so smooth
inside each other that I listen—before and after, without translation.
Nostalgia, heal my lacuna. I'm porous, away from loose ends and
against injury, mindful of boundaries like now or tongues set free. No
one can gauge how long it will take to outlast this benediction. Water
in plural, moments flicker so simply that when you say you are my old
mailbox, a familiar tanka to anchor reverie, I look for a sign to
renounce our blind rain.

NOT MEANT AS POEMS

I   Power in a Crystal Sarcophagus

Like Kim Il-sung.
Like Marcos.
Like Lenin.

Behind his glossy face, he tears at his own skin.

Sons,
take an oath
to his embalmed blood, a frozen sea
at the mercy of its sun.

He eats fear.
He rapes fear.
He sweet-talks fear.
He markets fear.

Walk in circles. No whisper. No pictures.

Are you scheming? *[To kill or to shield?]*
Will you go on strike? *[For a safe past or future?]*

No big deal.
Free your langue de bois.
No one will meddle, no army
summoned.
Political tracts as state souvenir—
they cite from *Time Out* and the Upanishads—
free of charge,

red ones at the first checkpoint,
brown ones at the exit.

I am not a journalist
or part-time activist, I come here
on a whim, of free will.
For a poem . . .
Down with spectators!
Shame on curiosity!
Just look innocent and let the beast
sleep—more
and more visitors
sweating and grunting
like hippopotamuses in a private bioreserve.

II   Putin's Dog

can't bark.

Putin's dog
can't jump
from a lofty height.

Putin's dog
can't fornicate
with other bourgeois dogs

on a winter stroll
in the Tsaritsyno Park.

Putin's dog
can't beg,
but is groomed,
spoilt,
and fed. With what—

I have no idea, neither
does the press.

Putin's dog
can't fire
its master
or look sick.
It won't suffer

beating or torture,
but can't sleep
without having to hide.

But Putin's dog, like
all dogs, can
(thank God)
pee-pee
or caca
whenever it likes.

III   Written in the Vernacular

Four a.m.
I fidget with a stone inkpot,

never empty, never filled.

                    *

Nothing in my song

        indicates despair. The rain of a world
        in late, organized joy.

                    *

Twofold agenda: a new strophe over the latent,

the pulse of reason writ into insufferable verbs.

                              *

Proper silence, that which is anti-point.

                              *

Without a window, the space has no weather.

                              *

List each anger—you won't live each trial twice.

                              *

To an unseen Buddha,
a mellow discourse,
hushed talk of lay nuns
[faces opaque, like mine, like yours]
who can't parry their belief
of an immortal system—is it about power
                              or morals—with or without hidden

                              surveillance,
two meals on weekends [usually corn flour bread],
long walks,
good deeds,
an elusive rat from chair to chair.

                              *

To quote Solzhenitsyn, *Blah blah blah* . . .

Tsvetaeva, *Nnh, nnh, nnh* . . .

I delete violence from words that fly too soon.

V

CHILD, DON'T HIDE

THE ILLUSION OF TENDERNESS

Narcissus in a Raku tea bowl—one you thought you
    saw in a private museum, on loan from Kyoto for undisclosed
reasons—floated on matcha from a thousand dinners
    back, forced by gravity to let go of stillness the moment

each petal floated on its terms, most
    dramatically, roughing out the principle of least action,
listening hands down to the chorus, *L-o-o-k.*

AGRIPPINA THE YOUNGER

I have no poems on maternity.

In an Asian culture, that's a sin, a one-
way ticket to Hades.

Of her voice, I feel it
before I bleed.
Monthly: against the grain and scrap.

Of her scheme, I remember:
Be grateful,
but know how to be mean. Nothing a classicist can do to force
her to admit *Yes,*
I said these.

I wish men would say *I forgive you*
and your cruelty. But when sagas are revised for sense and clarity,

gods can't forgive

the scandal *I forgive.*

MUSE, IF I

idealized you without knowing why, the man
or woman in a photograph from the warfront
would metamorphose into a whale or luffa. The winter
that broke down twice before someone smart
unplugged it overnight
would goose-bump your skin and freeze your toes and sterilize
your milk, your ovum or sperm. My typewriter
passed out from a crime
(details omitted because of the wife), rattled out my
silence about a Dutch spy, in
an apartment tapped by the mafia. If
I idealized you knowing why I should—not for a scenario, paid
by the line—I wouldn't triumph
with a healthy heart. It had pumped too fast
for the price you asked.

GIVE UP THINKING TWICE

I
[Acoustic]

Instead of Cohen, I heard another bard.
Some thought him thunder, some found him uphill.
So what if rain must fall hard, one grumbled.
Cut inside each chord, but surrendered for time.

Some thought him thunder, some found him uphill.
I listened to each repetition, an apology in the fewest words.
Cut inside each chord, but surrendered for time.
I would have given up a mountain for this storm.

I listened to each repetition, an apology in the fewest words.
How long it could last, it might have sensed when void of its heaven,
                                                it must fight its own earth.
I would have given up a mountain for this storm.
I credited the wind for his cri du cœur, discredited the same wind for his rhythm.

How long it could last, it might have sensed when void of its heaven,
                                                it must fight its own earth.
How much delirium to be heard as a poem, he did not answer.
                                        Did not bother.
I credited the wind for his cri du cœur, discredited the same wind for his rhythm.
To clarify music was not his task.

How much delirium to be heard as a poem, he did not answer.
                                        Did not bother.
Some thought it ego, some said he pushed notes off their high-speed rail.
To clarify music was not his task.

82

I saw a door when he played harmonica.

Some thought it ego, some said he pushed notes off their high-speed rail.
Green-blue and ajar.
I saw a door when he played harmonica.
No one waited behind or outside.

Green-blue and ajar.
Times changed its size—the door, not his mouthpiece or unplugged version.
No one waited behind or outside.
I could drink the drums had he not turned his back on us.

Times changed its size—the door, not his mouthpiece or unplugged version.
The troubadour aged fast not because of drugs.
I could drink the drums had he not turned his back on us.
I drew this theory from his Nobel prize. How he took his time.

The troubadour aged fast not because of drugs.
Heartbreak can be lean and acoustic. Like a piece of meat,
                                        if mood detained the beast.
I drew this theory from his Nobel prize. How he took his time.
Every song: a friend and moon to compete for its *chi* and wives.

Heartbreak can be lean and acoustic. Like a piece of meat,
                                        if mood detained the beast.
Sick of the word "love," it plagiarized the best failure.
Every song: a friend and moon to compete for its *chi* and wives.
Unlike a friend, it did not need to try hard.

Sick of the word "love," it plagiarized the best failure.
Unlike a moon, it spoke through the graves and diaspora.
Unlike a friend, it did not need to try hard.
Some gave up despair to find his past, some gave up even when alive.

Unlike a moon, it spoke through the graves and diaspora.
Years down the road, if words fell apart, this prophecy would ask
                                        for one odd star—

Some gave up despair to find his past, some gave up even when alive.
None of his demons survived their trance, none of this passion

                              leveled its height.

Years down the road, if words fell apart, this prophecy would ask

                              for one odd star—

So what if rain must fall hard, one grumbled.
None of his demons survived their trance, none of this passion

                              leveled its height.

Instead of Cohen, I heard another bard.

II
[Electric]

Instead of Cohen, I heard another bard.
Some thought him thunder, some found him uphill.
So what if rain must fall hard, one grumbled.
Cut inside each chord, but surrendered
for time. I listened to each repetition, an apology
in the fewest words. I would have given up a mountain
for this storm. How long it could last, it might
have sensed when void of its heaven,
it must fight its own earth. I credited the wind
for his cri du cœur, discredited the same
wind for his rhythm. How much delirium to be heard
as a poem, he did not answer. Did not bother.
To clarify music was not his task. Some thought
it ego, some said he pushed notes off their high
speed rail. I saw a door when he played harmonica.
Green-blue and ajar. No one waited behind or outside.
Times changed its size—the door, not his mouthpiece
or unplugged version. I could drink the drums had
he not turned his back on us. The troubadour aged
fast not because of drugs. I drew this theory
from his Nobel prize. How he took his time.
Heartbreak can be lean and acoustic. Like a piece

of meat, if mood detained the beast.
Every song: a friend and moon to compete
for its *chi* and wives. Sick of the word "love," it
plagiarized the best failure. Unlike a friend, it did
not need to try hard. Unlike a moon, it spoke through
the graves and diaspora. Some gave up despair to find
his past, some gave up even when alive. Years down
the road, if words fell apart, this prophecy would ask
for one odd star—none of his demons survived
their trance, none of this passion leveled its height.

> *Now the moon is almost hidden*
> *The stars are beginning to hide*
> *The fortune-telling lady*
> *Has even taken all her things inside*
> *All except for Cain and Abel*
> *And the hunchback of Notre Dame*
> *Everybody is making love*
> *Or else expecting rain*
> *And the Good Samaritan, he's dressing*
> *He's getting ready for the show . . .*

SIX PLAINSONGS

A former French President has put on weight.

I am halfway through the conceptual, any form of abstract expressionism.

   *

Good citizens are in need of new beds, another sleep pattern.

   *

Our wine has aged.
I sip at it,
One, two, three . . .
as if counting wounded birds.

   *

Listen to the bass
in Amy Winehouse, a tattoo that snakes through
arms and breasts,

a horizon

across a sunrise.
Or sunset, if you don't need the light.

   *

What am I thinking when I see a rose?

A magnified sperm
          growing its wings, petal
                    by petal, before combustion.

          *

What do I see when I think of a rose?

The self-destruction of a philosopher-bee.

THE SAYING AND THE SAID:
VENTRILOQUISTIC CLOUD CHRONICLES

I   **A Nonreligious Retreat**

[Enter three players. They speak at the same time.]

PLAYER A
You don't need to socialize. Not even at night.

PLAYER B
I've met the ghost who robbed Orpheus of his manhood.

PLAYER C
No comment about your happiness.

On day one, I ate like a nun:
    no meat, no wine. Eager to sleep and Skype someone.

The next day, I carpooled downtown
    for a toothbrush—ready to reform my inner life.

On day three, rain checked out of its grand hotel.

I became one of the evergreens, soon to look alike, and not cry.

II Sunday

At noon I ate a kiwi.

Seeds,
visible from the start.
No one knew
the backstreet down my throat.

A taste connected to the pin
in my liver. Of yielding.
The toughest pearl.
To an improper body, the same
old sunshine.

Even with French wine
and two silences,
thirst lingered.

I couldn't rise to the occasion.

*

I couldn't rise to the occasion.

Thirst lingered. And two silences.
Even with French wine, the same old sunshine.

To an improper body, the toughest pearl.
Of yielding. In my liver,

a taste connected to the pin, the backstreet
down my throat. No one knew—

visible from the start:

seeds. At noon I ate a kiwi.

III   Out of Context

I see a door in a Bonnard, now a museum

        of violet, mint, vermilion. The sun is caught in bed
and pajamas, keen for a shower and lotion.

        In a younger Bonnard, I see a taxpayer whose wife

runs around for grapes, clementines, and salad
        greens. The vitamins I buy from a peasant woman.

        Next to a neighbor who drugs his palate, my
evenings feel more liberal: Abbé Liszt, a Swedish

        film—monologues to pontify the lack of resources.

I have an issue with money this year. Lamp

        at each flicker an orange alert: out of work
        I empty my reserves, eat in decimals, recycle

        light bulbs from Cuba. *Soon thirty-five,* my father
whines, *yet no son. Do you have any talent?* Answer:

        I wait for love. His, for instance. When I think too

much, I leave the door open. Like in a Bonnard,
        one of the above: a wife who does laundry at break-

fast, the idealist who reconstructs a fruit from winter.

IV I Titled This Poem "Masque for the Noble, the Rich,
the Elite" Because I Failed to Name My Characters

What are your origins? Strangers glare
                through my skin. I hear myself
lying at half price. Eye
                the fattest piece of apple strudel.
Why win an argument? *My country*
                code is 33. Someone delves
into my thoughts, *Too accurate*
                for a riddle. Spectacles fall.
Faces of male guests, raw
                potatoes. *Do you suffer from anorexia?*

One jokes about *Out of Africa*
                and Eileen Chang's novella
"Red Rose, White Rose."
                I haven't read it, but watched the film.
A prince is here for a speech
                on tea culture. Freud has a term
for every behavior: sublimation.
                The pleasure principle. Waiters
aren't spared from the case studies.
                Like ostriches, spinsters parade.

Unlike ostriches, spinsters do not run
                away. I am hungry. My appetite
is Greek. *Can Thai food make*
                money? asks a divorcé who wags
a leg. Like an egg, his bald head.
                X protests, *No Muslim food.*
Y replies, *Not for free meals.*
                Hard to laugh when X and Y,
once religious, evoke religion,
                while they fail to a. control

their children; b. flush the toilet.

        I am a print media at this benefit.
Someone insists I share my ancestors.

        A shamaness burned for her people,
I say I starved in a plateau with my kind.

        My gods are Macedonian. They teach
me to bow, sweep off the dust, find

        the right words before the treasure.
How intriguing! The mayor raises her

        eyebrows, *We're fundraising for diversity.*

V   Qualitative Anatomy

I imitate Alda Merini—

narcissism,
not in the title.

Facts borrowed from a health record:

"A woman smart enough to replace 'I' with 'We.'
Her ego the size of an overrated moon."

VI   WeTransfer

At the airport, I looked
for a heart
past each arrival
and hour
of departure,
away from the crowd
and upbeat couples
with nothing special
to tell each other,
yet unable to yield
to the instant
or stay out
of each other's
field of vision.
Anywhere could run
as a sequel
or pattern
or an abstract play
in various languages.
Without a cushion, I felt
its tension—
the airport's skeleton
and its nervous
system. Cities digested,
heavens downloaded.
I observed not
humans, but shoes,
cigarettes, duty-free
liquor landing
in bags
of nondualism—
arrived
or in-transit,
from left to right,
hand-carried

but to be tagged,
except one,
not for two in three—
flexing their muscles
when each announcement
injected a new
shot of insulin
and dope
into the veins of this
hooked animal.

THE GREAT WALL OF CHINA

a zuihitsu for Kafka

Dogdom is a word I masticate. Its virtues, I lap and swallow in a gulp.

The mouse does not always win in a fable. Its role: waiting for the cat to take on the villain act.
[Read *The Guardian* and *The New York Times*: at No. 10, Larry the cat stays while the Prime Minister goes.]

The Sirens haunt Ulysses in the audience because *it is conceivable that someone might possibly have escaped from their singing; but from their silence certainly never.*

More dog laws, more humans.

My cage did not go in search of a bird. I had cleaned the cage with detergent.

Who is the Evil One?
I bring a message uniquely for him—typed out on a letterhead from JP Morgan Chase, font size nine, font type Monaco.

Theoretically, none of these books exists in happiness, yet they can't be nullified by the very indestructible element in themselves.

"He"/"She"—
do not keep associating "him"/"her" with "intercourse,"
physical and spiritual.

Much of the experience deals with accepting the sin rather than the sinner.

[This speaks for lovers, couples, hookers and pimps, doctors and nurses . . . in 1920, as well as before or after that monkey year.]

Remind me for the last time: does A. add pepper to every omelette, then separate the green ones from the red?
I ask because he does not eat with a fork.

How long the burrow runs depends not on my will, though it does reach the Castle Keep somehow. Still, isn't the burrow the Castle Keep?

The appetite for life. An appetite for thirst.

I imagine the hunter Gracchus piloting his death ship before hell broke loose, since he couldn't know the ship was perfectly capable of cruising through earthly waters, and it was better to sail forward after his last breath.

What does Kafka have to say
about opposites—a rain streamlined by toxins,
                a mist that Brontë tore off her page?

[All three Brontës have driven out the weather, without regard for the past or future.]

Not sure about *not dying along with one's dying thoughts* . . .

A rope.
A crow.
An unbiased context.

The fragment about two antagonists who live inside him—one pushing him from behind, the other blocking the path before him—strikes him as a dream that stops right before both run out of energy battling each other. "Both" as in him and one of the antagonists—never two antagonists in direct confrontation—such as the dream exists just as a dream within a dream, and stops as a dream within a dream.

A crow.
A rope.
A biased write-up.

We must be ready at every moment—especially after the year 1920. After the Great War. And its bipolar horses.

This is how translation fails for a mainstream audience:
a. A playwright I translate goes in search of a cage for her theater.
b. I went in search of a cage for her own bird.

An Austrian family hired a doorkeeper before they traveled abroad. The doorkeeper spoke Czech and German. He took the job because he needed the cash, even though he was afraid of their dog. Thank God it stayed in the yard, not indoors. Whenever he opened the door for their postman, he stuck to the same thought in Czech and German: *Please, no dog.*

Frau Milena, did you really enjoy being a foreigner? Or just in Vienna?

. . . and in a few weeks one will be in America—suddenly, I would like something hot. Something that tells me, the taste can turn into furniture music.

As of November 2014, I live in dogdom and pray for scientists.

The problem isn't you. I too have never visited a zoo.

SELF-PORTRAIT AS A LANDSCAPE WITHOUT ITS MEMORIES AND MY AGE

Oil and gouache on canvas
30½ x 25 in.

Color to begin as a vertical verse: a reach for pure
sugar, a route
to pleasure and the quiet.
Edible petals stare upward,
plain—
enough to ask for praise.
Mauve, ruby, shades of beaver or carmine,
outpacing the light,
angled and troubled on the fringe
of what must shut.

Let dust settle on a broader pier, clarity
fastened at eye level.
Bare elements—each buoyed
up to mid-horizon
                    on the verge of waste,
like a high note from a portable radio, sorting
its way through. More bees, more.
The horizon backtracks for precision.
Rising silk dresses carry dispatches.
Arousing birth, they whisper
                    circle circle, and circle: the first
of few secrets in a pirouette.

Eddies of leaf-shadow, the mood
                              for fallen smoke.

Fond of shelter and the upturned
earth, air in a grain, each suggestion real.
Windbeaten into a tree after
                    a worm posture.
Folded or apart, the scent brews luck,
out for itself and seduced by fingers. When
was the last time
we inhaled like strings, a bowl of herbs,

                              palms half-open to wild
ingredients? Nothing of this moment
survives as error.
Fat lizard gone, a ladder
and a pod.
Child, don't hide—
                    I can touch your nose, ten degrees of rain,
breath withdrawn to hear each frog
drinking loops of hair.

ETERNITY

How does one define spirit
without blood
to make the body known across a shore
so point-blank
that we see its passing tail? Once
                    of stone,
        before a winter moon,
the spirit moves from one width to the next height, lighter
than the sweet failure
                    of wind and hours and a stranded sail.

Spirit, I don't tell myself you control our field,
        the random face
        of a god who leaves us old,
        an alley to somewhere hypnotic,
        prolonged
        and curved at each turn.
                    When you come, you ask the same question
            I commit to poor speech—
            how places grieve poised in distance,
            while the rest of us die
            trying to live.
                    When you leave, you offer nothing
            but the reason to fade, that it is beyond you to respond to silence,
            after the cold, when pain
            outwears pain
            and quantum physics.
I don't tell
a soul—what you intuit

on a peak. I won't tell others how storms heal
       or stop the countdown,
why echoes blink
to preserve the drift.
I won't paint your dream in this portrait.

NOTES

The Problem with Music

The guzheng or zheng is an ancient Chinese zither that has existed since the fifth century B.C. The modern zheng contains twenty-one strings, each with its own movable wooden bridge.

A Matter of Time

I am unable to ascertain my grandmother's year of birth: 1921 or 1927?

After Being Loved

The stanza by William Blake is from his poem "The Human Abstract" in *Songs of Experience* (1794), the second collection of *Songs of Innocence and of Experience* (1789–1794).

Preface to a Cloud Chronicle

Kazuo Dan (1912–1976) and Osamu Dazai (1909–1948) are among the most significant twentieth-century Japanese writers.

Mimesis: Cloud Chronicle

Tatsumi Hijikata (1928–1986) was recognized as one of the founders of butoh. In 1959, he created the first butoh work, *Kinjiki*. Sankai Juku is a world-renowned butoh dance company founded by Ushio Amagatsu in 1975. This poem is based on Sankai Juku's performance of *Hibiki* (1998)—a butoh creation by Amagatsu—during the 2002 Next Wave Festival at the Brooklyn Academy of Music.

11

"The Jewish Giant" refers to a photograph of the "giant" entertainer Eddie Carmel (1936–1972) by Diane Arbus in 1970. It was taken "at home with his parents in the Bronx, New York." According to what I read online, Carmel was seven feet, three inches tall.

Arbus wrote, "I know a Jewish giant who lives in Washington Heights or the Bronx with his little parents. He is tragic with a curious bitter somewhat stupid wit. The parents are orthodox and repressive and classic and disapprove of his carnival career. . . . They are a truly metaphorical family."

[Postcard from Diane Arbus to Peter Crookston, circa May 1968—see Sandra S. Phillips's essay "The Question of Belief" in *Diane Arbus Revelations* (Jonathan Cape, 2003), 67.]

The Reality of a Nightmare

The line by Jorge Luis Borges comes from his poem "Doomsday," translated from the Spanish by Stephen Kessler in *Poems of the Night* (Penguin Books, 2010).

Wolinski 1934–2015

French cartoonist Georges Wolinski was murdered with eight other *Charlie Hebdo* colleagues, two police officers, and a building maintenance worker on January 7, 2015 during the terrorist attack on *Charlie Hebdo*. He was eighty.

Four months later, two hundred and four PEN writers created a "polemic" by "protesting" against the Freedom of Expression Courage Award conferred on *Charlie Hebdo* by PEN America.

Strand

American poet Mark Strand (1934–2014) spent his final years making collages in Madrid. He died in Brooklyn, two days after Thanksgiving.

Nine Solitudes
[When you reach the Academy of Ruins]

My source for the quotation is *Oxford Treasury of Sayings and Quotations*, edited by Susan Ratcliffe (Oxford University Press, 1997; fourth ed., 2011), 281.

[After a year of clairvoyance, the river]

The opening excerpt is from "Discovered" in Edith Södergran's *We Women*, translated from the Swedish and the German by Samuel Charters (Tavern Books, 2015).

Sea Ballads

The quotation by Edward Thomas in "Black Hour" is from the chapter "History and the Parish—Hampshire—Cornwall" in Thomas's *The South Country*, first published by Richard Clay and Sons in 1909.

Give Up Thinking Twice

The italicized excerpt at the end of this poem is from the third stanza of Bob Dylan's closing track "Desolation Row" for his *Highway 61 Revisited* (1965).

The Saying and the Said: Ventriloquistic Cloud Chronicles
V   Qualitative Anatomy

The revered Italian poet Alda Merini (1931–2009) wrote an eight-line poem named after herself in "La gazza ladra. Venti ritratti" ("The Thieving Magpie: Twenty Portraits," 1985), translated by Susan Stewart in Merini's selected poems *Love Lessons* (Princeton, 2009).

The Great Wall of China

This poem contains notes on some of Franz Kafka's stories, fables, and aphorisms in *The Great Wall of China: Stories and Reflections* (Schocken Books, 1948), translated from the German by Willa and Edwin Muir, as well as parts of Kafka's correspondence in *Letters to Milena* (Vintage, 1999), edited by Willy Haas and translated by Tania and James Stern.

ACKNOWLEDGMENTS

Several poems, often in earlier form, first found a home in *Antigonish Review, Antioch Review, Bitter Oleander, Jacket2 Supplement, Michigan Quarterly Review, Paris Lit Up, Pearl, Poetry Ireland, Poetry London, Poetry Northwest, Prairie Schooner, Salmagundi,* and *The Literary Review.*

"Not Meant as Poems" appeared in a handmade chapbook of limited edition from The Green Violin in Montreal in 2018.
"Written in the Vernacular" appeared in *A Blue Dark*, a joint exhibition with Fritz Horstman at the Institute Library (The Gallery Upstairs) in New Haven, Connecticut, from June to September 2019.

My gratitude goes to the Columbia Institute for Ideas and Imagination. I must acknowledge the Bergman Estate and MALBA, and thank the Helene Wurlitzer Foundation, Writers Omi, and Yaddo for their hospitality and resources.

To Susan Stewart, Natasha Sajé, Christina Cook, William Merwin, and Mark Strand: my respect and affection.

Princeton Series of Contemporary Poets